HAUNTED DARTMOOR

A GHOST-HUNTER'S GUIDE

R. W. Bamberg

Illustrations by George Thurlow

'I counsel you by way of caution to forbear from crossing the moor in those dark hours when the powers of evil are exalted.'

Sir Arthur Conan Doyle: *The Hound of the Baskervilles*

Peninsula
Press

First published in 1993 by Peninsula Press Ltd
P.O. Box 31
Newton Abbot
Devon TQ12 5XH

Reprinted 2000

British Library Cataloguing in Publication Data

A catalogue record for this book is available from the British Library.

ISBN 1 872640 25 7

Printed and bound in Great Britain by:
Kingfisher Print & Design Ltd, Totnes, Devon TQ9 5XN

Sales and Distribution by:
Forest Publishing, Woodstock, Liverton, Newton Abbot,
Devon TQ12 6JJ (Tel: 01626 821631)

CONTENTS

INTRODUCTORY NOTES

SOME ADVICE

1. Do not take young children or those of a nervous disposition on these excursions.

2. Do not go alone but in pairs or larger groups, as the presence of corroborative witnesses is important if a manifestation is experienced.

3. A dog makes a comforting companion and may become aware of sights or sounds invisible or inaudible to human senses, but it should be kept firmly on a lead at all times.

4. Restrict your expeditions to the summer months, May to September, when the weather is warmer and the light better.

5. Time your expeditions to coincide with either dusk or dawn. Make midnight excursions only to those sites which are within a hundred metres of the spot where you have parked the car.

6. Make sure your car is securely locked when left in the car park.

7. Take note of the weather forecast before you leave. If it is likely to be cold, wet or windy, postpone your expedition until the weather prospects are more favourable.

TAKE WITH YOU

The double-sided Ordnance Survey 1:25000 Outdoor Leisure Map of Dartmoor (South Sheet 28a & North Sheet 28b) to which the Grid References (WE followed by SN) at the head of each Section refer. Plenty of warm, waterproof and brightly-coloured clothing. Even during high summer Dartmoor can be extremely cold, and the weather conditions are notoriously unpredictable. Sleeping bags and ground-sheets. Food: hot soup and coffee in thermos flasks, with 'iron rations' (chocolate, dried fruit, biscuits) at least. A torch, a watch, a whistle, a compass and a pair of binoculars. A tape recorder, a still camera with flash attachment and, if you have one, a video camera. A pen and notebook to record your observations.

TUNHILL KISTVAEN, BLACKSLADE DOWN

THE DEVIL'S RENDEZVOUS

LOCATION

OS 1:25000 Outdoor Leisure Map, South Sheet 28a: Grid Ref. 734755
2 km./1 mile SE of WIDECOMBE; 7 km./4 miles NW of ASHBURTON

APPROACH BY ROAD

From ASHBURTON (6 km./3 miles): leave the town via North Street, turn left over the bridge and follow the road uphill. Take the right turn signposted Widecombe, across the cattle grid and continue straight on at the first cross-roads at Cold East Cross. A short distance beyond the cross-roads you will see a track leading down to your left. Park here.

ACCESS (1 km./½ mile)

Follow the track down, across the ford and up the further slope. The low, irregular mound of Tunhill Kistvaen is situated some 20 m. to the right of the track, at the point where it reaches its highest elevation and almost due south of the summit of Pil Tor.

THE LEGEND

Tunhill, or Blackslade, Kistvaen (marked as a 'Cairn and Cist' on the OS map) is a Bronze Age tomb in which the cremated remains of a prehistoric warrior were once interred. Crossing, writing in 1909, states that the kistvaen (a 'fine example') had been 'discovered several years ago buried beneath a cairn', but little can now be discerned of the original structure. Four granite slabs form the sides of the small rectangular box in which the ashes were placed: but the lid is missing, and the stones which once ringed and covered it have been scattered. Those which remain are half-hidden in turf, gorse and heather.

This insignificant mound is said to be the spot where, on the 21st of October 1631, Jan Reynolds the tinner was accosted by a sinister hooded (or masked - in any case the face was invisible) stranger and persuaded to sell his soul in return for seven years' good fortune as a gambler. Tradition relates that, the seven years having passed, Satan reappeared to claim his prize one Sunday afternoon as Jan slept through a service in Widecombe church, announcing his arrival with a flash of lightning and a clap of thunder. While the congregation sat stunned and terror-stricken the hapless victim was seized, dragged to the top of the tower and carried away on a huge black horse. Tunhill Kistvaen, then, is one of those spots where the foolish, the foolhardy or the greedy may be lured to damnation with a signature scrawled in their own blood.

Note: That local tradition associates this particular area with Satanic activity is supported by two further pieces of evidence. Pil Tor and the prehistoric enclosures of Foale's Arrishes (see NEWHOUSE INN) lie only a few hundred metres distant N and NE from the site. Crossing writes: 'It was at Foale's Arrishes that a certain villager once decided to settle, and though his neighbours tried to persuade him to remain where he was, set out one day with the avowed intention of erecting a shelter on the spot and passing the remainder of his days there. But ... the labourer was never seen again. Whether he was spirited away by the pixies, or fell a prey to the Evil One, who was said to take an airing occasionally on (Pil) Tor Hill, on the slope of which the Arrishes are situated, nobody could say; all that was certain was that the neighbourhood knew him no more'. He also states that the stone cross cut in a granite slab on nearby Rippon Tor was probably carved 'in the belief that the holy symbol would free the spot from heathen superstitions'.

NEWHOUSE INN, HEMSWORTHY GATE

PHANTOM HORSEMAN

LOCATION

OS 1:25000 Outdoor Leisure Map, South Sheet 28a: Grid Ref. 741756
2.5 km./1½ miles SE of WIDECOMBE; 7 km./4 miles NW of ASHBURTON

APPROACH BY ROAD

From ASHBURTON (7 km./4 miles): Follow the directions given for TUNHILL KISTVAEN, but continue past the track to your left for a further km. or so. Before you reach the next cross-roads (Hemsworthy Gate) you will arrive at a pair of stone gate-posts on your left. The ruins of Newhouse Inn, a scatter of squared granite blocks and a few wind-warped trees stand in a grassy area enclosed by low turf walls behind the gate-posts. You can park on the site.

ACCESS

You're there!

THE LEGEND

Crossing, writing in 1909, described the remains of Newhouse as 'scanty', consisting 'only of a few low walls marking the site of a dwelling, and some enclosures near it with a dozen weather-beaten thorn bushes'. Little has changed since his day except that the ruins are now yet more scattered and fragmentary. However, two other man-made relics and a natural formation close by may have some bearing on the sinister reputation which the stretch of road between Hemsworthy Gate and Cold East Cross has acquired. North-west of Newhouse, on the slopes of Pil Tor, the pattern of small fields known as 'Foale's Arrishes' (see TUNHILL KISTVAEN) may be discerned: within and around these enclosures are the remains of several Bronze Age hut circles, evidence of a farm worked there perhaps three thousand years ago; just to the north of Hemsworthy Gate and close to the road stands the jumbled cairn of Seven Lords' Lands, a prehistoric barrow; and immediately below Foale's Arrishes, between Newhouse and Pil Tor, lies the expanse of Blackslade Mire, with its treacherous marshes and eerie will o' wisps.

This particular stretch of road between Hemsworthy Gate and Cold East Cross seems quite unremarkable, but according to rumour a horseman, or possibly a coach and horses, has been witnessed travelling along it at break-neck speed but absolutely silently on certain still and moonlit nights. Sometimes the rider (or coachman) is headless, sometimes his silver hair is seen streaming behind him; and one report describes him as wearing an old-fashioned frogged military tunic or greatcoat.

Before the coming of the turnpikes this road, though then only a rough upland track, was a busy one, linking Ashburton with Chagford, Bovey Tracey and Moretonhampstead - hence the presence of the isolated Newhouse Inn, which burnt down in mysterious circumstances some 150 years ago. Perhaps the legend perpetuates the memory of some long-forgotten highwayman who once frequented the neighbourhood; perhaps the burning down of the inn has some significance, for some versions of the story suggest that the spectral figure slows or stops as it passes the ruin before quickening its pace once more; perhaps the ghost (if one discounts the 'tunic' sighting) emerges at night from its lair in the barrow or among the ancient hut circles. Was a wandering horseman sucked down beneath the swamps of Blackslade Mire one dark night long ago? Or did the marsh-lights flickering over its surface deceive the eyes of a lonely traveller on the road and lure him to his doom?

SQUIRE CABELL'S TOMB, BUCKFASTLEIGH CHURCH

HAUNTED GRAVE

LOCATION

OS 1:25000 Outdoor Leisure Map, South Sheet 28a: Grid Ref. 743666
1 km./ ½ mile N of BUCKFASTLEIGH

APPROACH BY ROAD

From BUCKFASTLEIGH (1 km./ ½ mile): though it is possible to reach the peculiarly isolated church on foot up a long flight of steps, it is much easier to get there by car. Take the road running north out of the village through Lower Town then fork right up Church Hill. Park by the churchyard gate.

ACCESS

Enter the churchyard and approach the church. The small stone building to the left of the path by the church porch contains the tomb.

THE LEGEND

Buckfastleigh Church has been associated with devil-worship for many centuries and the practice seems to have continued till the present day. Over the past few years the church has been subject to numerous attacks allegedly by Satanists performing black magic rituals, these attacks culminating in a recent (1992) fire in which the interior was practically gutted. Only the shell now remains, and at the time of writing it is doubtful whether the building will ever be restored.

The origins of this tradition seem to go back to the time of Squire Cabell, a great huntsman and monstrously evil man who was reputed to have sold his soul to the Devil. When he died in 1677 he was buried in the churchyard of Buckfastleigh, but his tormented spirit cannot rest. On dark, stormy nights phantom hounds surround his tomb; the sounds of lamentation - wailing, shrieking and an unearthly howling - fill the air. A flickering red glow and the shadows of bars are cast on the church wall as if a fire has been lit in the tomb. Some say Satan's minions gather here to carry away the Squire's soul; others that his ghost emerges from the tomb to hunt, with this black spectral pack, along a nearby ancient track known as the Abbot's Way. To glimpse the phantom will mean death within the year.

The building by the church porch, through the wrought-iron railing of which you can see Squire Cabell's flat-topped rectangular tomb with its half-obliterated Latin inscription, was constructed by local people in an attempt to contain the spectre and thus prevent its escape. Belief in the legend certainly persisted until recent times, for a suggestion made during World War II that the railing be removed for scrap met with such opposition from local people that the scheme had to be abandoned.

Note (1): The legend of Squire Cabell seems to have formed the basis of Conan Doyle's famous Dartmoor story *The Hound of the Baskervilles*. Cabell's house at Brook Manor (west of Buckfastleigh) possibly served as the original for Baskerville Hall, though Heatree House near Manaton is a more likely model from the topographical point of view. Also, there is an odd similarity between the tale of Squire Cabell and Count Magnus, one of M. R. James's *Ghost Stories of an Antiquary*, which is also concerned with a haunted tomb from which an evil spirit escapes.

Note (2): If you walk round the church, be sure to do so in a clockwise direction: for it is said that if a person travels 'widdershins' they will encounter the devil peering out at them from the church porch.

CROCKERN TOR, TWO BRIDGES

SPECTRAL FIGURE

LOCATION

OS 1:25000 Outdoor Leisure Map, North Sheet 28b: Grid Ref. 616757
1 km./ $\frac{1}{2}$ mile NE of TWO BRIDGES; 2.5 km./ $1\frac{1}{2}$ miles NE of PRINCETOWN

APPROACH BY ROAD

From PRINCETOWN (2.5 km./ $1\frac{1}{2}$ miles): take the B3212 (signposted Two Bridges). At the T-junction, turn right along the B3357 (signposted Dartmeet). Cross the bridge over the West Dart, then fork left along the B3212 (signposted Postbridge and Moretonhampstead). Park on the grass verge just beyond the first house on your left (Parson's Cottage).

ACCESS (0.4 km./ $\frac{1}{4}$ mile)

A farm gate on the left just by your parking place gives access to the short, steep footpath leading up to the summit of Crockern Tor, which can be seen clearly from the road.

THE LEGEND

Were it not for its historical and legendary significance, Crockern Tor would be 'nothing remarkable', as it consists 'only of a small group of rocks' and attains 'an elevation of no more than 1295 feet' (Crossing). However, this eminence - placed as it is in the very centre of Dartmoor - was from mediaeval times until the eighteenth century the meeting place of the Stannary Parliament, which administered the local tin industry. At one time the summit was equipped with stone seats for the use of the delegates, but few relics of its former function now remain. The site is believed to be haunted by 'Old Crockern', a spectral figure mounted upon a skeleton horse, who emerges from his fastness among the rocks at midnight to journey across the moor. It is said that the rider, 'grey as granite, and his eyebrows hanging down over his glimmering eyes like sedge, and his eyes deep as peat water pools', wields a gleaming sword or scythe, while the bones of his skeletal steed glimmer with a pale greenish luminescence. The approach of the ghost is heralded by a rush of icy wind, the dry rattle of bones, the clatter of falling masonry and a thin eerie whistling sound.

Note (1): It may well be that the story of Old Crockern has been confused with the legend of Wistman's Wood, a grove of dwarf oaks growing amidst a jumble of boulders along the near bank of the River Dart a couple of kilometres to the north of Crockern Tor. The legend of the Dartmoor 'Yeth', 'Wish' or 'Whist' Hounds appears to be a version of the Norse 'Wild Hunt', a supernatural phenomenon in which Odin (identified with the Devil in Christian mythology) leads a band of homeless dead across the sky, to the terror of any mortal who witnesses it. The horned hunters ride black horses and are attended by huge black hounds with flaming, hideous eyes. It is evident from its name that Wistman's (from 'whist' ('eerie'), and the Celtic 'maen' or 'stone') Wood has been associated with Satanic practices since ancient times. According to the legend Dewer (the Devil) and his phantom pack set out from among the boulders of the wood as dusk falls, returning to their kennels of stone at dawn after their wild excursions across the moor (see DEWERSTONE ROCK).

Note (2): The footpath which crosses the moor along the slopes above Wistman's Wood is a stretch of the ancient Lych Way along which, in mediaeval times, corpses were carried on a fifteen mile journey from isolated farmsteads to Lydford churchyard (see COFFIN WOOD). This may also have some bearing on Crockern Tor's sinister reputation.

DEWERSTONE ROCK, SHAUGH PRIOR

THE WILD HUNT

LOCATION:

OS 1:25000 Outdoor Leisure Map, South Sheet 28a: Grid Ref. 538639
1 km./$^1/_2$ mile NW of SHAUGH PRIOR; 4 km./2 miles SE of YELVERTON

APPROACH BY ROAD

From YELVERTON (4 km./2 miles): just south of the A386 roundabout a left turn (signposted Cadover Bridge) will take you past the church. Follow the signs for Cadover Bridge until you see it in the valley below you. Park on the left, on the near side of the bridge.

ACCESS (2 km./1 mile)

Cross the road and bear right (uphill), keeping the wall to your left. Continue past a conspicuous U-shaped rock formation from which point the Dewerstone can be seen ahead of you. Walk down the dip and up the further slope. The Dewerstone is among the trees on your left.

THE LEGEND

This huge mass of rock overlooking the River Plym and plunging in a sheer hundred-metre cliff to the thickly-wooded gorge below, is one of the most dramatic natural features of Dartmoor and marks its southern boundary. The views are spectacular and the Iron Age fortress (see HUNTER'S TOR) which once stood on the site must have been well-nigh impregnable. A steep and rocky path does in fact lead down to the river near this point, but at the time of writing is too eroded to be negotiated in safety even by daylight. In any case, should you wish to explore the area in more detail, do so while the sun is still up: you should certainly resist any temptation to approach the edge during the hours of dusk or dawn.

If Wistman's Wood (see CROCKERN TOR) is the point from which the Wild Hunt starts and to which it returns, the Dewerstone (the Devil's Stone) is its destination. Victims - people lost and wandering on the moor - are driven by Dewer on his great black horse and his pack of Yeth or Whist Hounds over hill and down dale towards the edge of the cliff, where, in a state of exhaustion and terror, they fall from the precipice to be dashed on the rocks below. The approach of the hunt is heralded by the thunder of hoofs, the baying of the hounds and peals of hollow laughter, accompanied by lightning, thunder and the smell of brimstone. Another tradition maintains that the hunt itself vanishes over the cliff-edge, and that anyone foolish enough to attempt to follow meets with the same fate. It is related that a local shepherd, trudging home through the snow across Wigford Down one frosty winter's night when the moon was full, heard from the Dewerstone the sound of baying hounds and distant screams. He hurried to the edge of the cliff and peered over. Below him, silhouetted against the snow, he saw to his horror a pack of gigantic hounds devouring a body which lay stretched upon the rocks. When the hounds became aware of his presence they lifted their flaming eyes, threw back their heads and howled in triumph. The following morning a party of men from Shaugh Prior returned to the spot. The prints of naked human feet, horse-shoes, cloven hoofs and enormous paw-prints were found in the snow of the summit crag, but of the corpse at its foot there was no trace save an area of trampled snow stained with blood, and a tattered cloak.

Note: It may also be worth investigating Cadover Bridge itself, which seems to have been the site of some Celtic conflict ('cad' means 'battle' in that language) and is said to be haunted by the cries of invisible warriors and the clash of steel.

THE NINE MAIDENS, BELSTONE

THE WITCHES' SABBAT

LOCATION

OS Outdoor Leisure Map, North Sheet 28b: Grid Ref. 614928
1 km./ 1/2 mile SW of BELSTONE; 4 km./2 miles SE of OKEHAMPTON

APPROACH BY ROAD

From OKEHAMPTON (4 km./2 miles): take A30 Exeter road, then pass over the flyover and turn right for Belstone. Drive through the village, passing the church and the No Through Road sign until you reach a moor gate. Park here opposite the Water Treatment Works.

ACCESS (1 km./1/2 mile)

Go through the moor gate then follow the track beyond, keeping the wall to your right, then over the shoulder of Watchet Hill. As you descend towards the East Okement River you can see the Nine Stones circle away to your left on a rock-strewn slope about 100m. from the track.

THE LEGEND

The Nine Maidens (or Nine Stones) are the remnants of an unrestored Bronze Age barrow, the circle of seventeen stones representing the retaining wall of the burial chamber, or kistvaen, which once stood within it. Of the tomb itself, however, nothing remains but a slight depression (containing a small cairn) at the centre. The circle is some seven metres in diameter and, according to Pevsner (*The Buildings of England,* 1952) 'there is an unusual uniformity in the height of the principal stones'. Some of these have fallen and gaps indicate where others have been removed. The site, particularly at dusk, possesses a curiously melancholy atmosphere, partly on account of its bleak, isolated position and dilapidated state.

Why, when it consists of seventeen stones, is this circle known as the Nine Stones, or (locally), the Nine Maidens? And why is it said that a count of the stones never arrives at the same number twice? Crossing maintains that 'maiden' is a corruption of the Celtic 'maen', or 'stone': but the combination of 'nine' with 'maiden' suggests both a witches' coven of nine members and the nine forms of the witch-goddess, Hecate. Also, according to legend, the Nine Stones are the petrified figures of nine maidens, turned to stone as a punishment for dancing on the Sabbath but resurrected to dance again 'at every Hunter's Moon ... 'twixt dark of night and break of day'. It seems therefore that local tradition has invented the 'counting difficulty' to account for the discrepancy between nine and seventeen: and has substituted the harmless 'Sabbath' for the original 'sabbat', either out of superstitious dread or in order to conceal from outsiders the true significance of the place. The site is in fact the sacred spot where a coven of witches gathers to enact its 'sabbat' (or ritual ceremony) at each of the eight annual pagan festivals - Yule (winter solstice), Imbolc (31 January - 1 February), Ostara (vernal equinox), Beltane (30 April - 1 May), Litha (midsummer solstice), Lammas (31 July - 1 Aug), Mabon (autumnal equinox), and Samhain, or Hallowe'en (31 October - 1 November). As the only witch festivals to fall within the summer period are Litha and Lammas, I suggest that you plan your expedition accordingly.

Note: Dartmoor barrows are frequently associated with witchcraft. Worth (*Dartmoor,* 1953) writes: 'A fine kistvaen was unearthed in the centre of a sepulchral circle, and in a cavity in its north end were found two large coils of human hair. There is little doubt that this represents an act of attempted witchcraft in comparatively recent times'.

SCORHILL CIRCLE, GIDLEIGH

HUMAN SACRIFICE

LOCATION

OS 1:25000 Outdoor Leisure Map, North Sheet 28b: Grid Ref. 655874
5 km./3 miles W of CHAGFORD; 2 km./1 mile SW of GIDLEIGH

APPROACH BY ROAD

From CHAGFORD (4 km./2 miles): follow the signs for Gidleigh, but keep straight at the right turn for Gidleigh/Chapple, following the Berrydown/Scorhill sign. By-pass Berrydown and ignore the right turn to Creaber; instead drive past the No Through Road sign. Park by the moor gate opposite Scorhill Farm.

ACCESS (1 km./ ½ mile)

Go through the gate then uphill along the track beyond, keeping to the wall on your right. Where the wall bears sharply right continue straight on across the open moor, over the shoulder of the hill. As you descend the slope you will see Scorhill Circle below you and off to your right.

THE LEGEND

Scorhill Circle is not, like the Nine Stones (see THE NINE MAIDENS), the retaining wall of a vanished kistvaen, but a so-called 'sacred' circle, earlier in date than the latter, larger in scale and composed of bigger, more widely-spaced stones. The original function of such sites can only be guessed at, but their disc shape suggests that they may well have been temples connected with the worship of the sun. Certainly fires - sacrificial, crematory or ceremonial - were burned within the ring. Scorhill Circle is an unrestored example of the type and, with its diameter of twenty-five metres, the largest on Dartmoor. Of the original sixty-odd stones of which it was composed, thirty remain, twenty-three erect and seven fallen; they vary in height between one and two metres.

Three apparently unconnected legends point to the sinister significance of Scorhill Circle. It is said that promiscuous or unfaithful women were, in times past, forced to expiate their sins by kneeling and praying for forgiveness before one of the standing stones. If the petitioner's prayers were answered, the stone remained motionless, indicating that she was judged to be purged of her guilt: if her transgressions were considered too heinous for expiation the stone toppled slowly forward, crushing her to death beneath its massive bulk - hence the seven fallen stones beneath each of which lie, according to tradition, a female skeleton. Tradition also avers that the circle is the home of a giant (or troll) who preys on sheep in the vicinity, returning to the spot to cook and devour his kill. On dark nights his presence is signified by the flickering of fire between the stones, and the stench of roasting flesh. It is also said that the atmosphere of evil hanging over the place is so powerful that no horse or dog will consent to travel at night along the cart track which passes between the stones of the ring unless compelled to do so. According to Frazer (*The Golden Bough*) the Aztecs - also sun-worshippers - engaged in human sacrifice during their religious ceremonies, the victims being crushed to death between enormous blocks of stone. Thus the legends of Scorhill Circle may be the distorted folk memory of a time when ritual murders, followed by cannibalistic feasts, were enacted at the site. As for its sinister reputation, if one theory regarding the existence of ghosts - that the record of tragic or barbarous deeds somehow becomes 'imprinted' in the landscape where they occur - is correct, then it is no wonder that creatures particularly sensitive to the smell of blood should find the atmosphere of the place thoroughly disquieting.

PIXIES' HOUSE
SHEEPS TOR

HAUNTED CAVE

LOCATION

OS 1:25000 Outdoor Leisure Map, South Sheet 28a: Grid Ref. 566681
4.5 km./2½ miles E of YELVERTON; 1 km./½ mile NE of SHEEPSTOR VILLAGE

APPROACH BY ROAD

From YELVERTON (4.5 km./2½ miles): from the A386 roundabout, take the B3212 signposted Princetown. Turn right in Dousland, following the signs for Sheepstor across the dam and through the village. Beyond Sheepstor turn left past the MoD sign and continue until you reach the open moor. Sheep's Tor is above you to the left. Park here.

ACCESS (0.5 km./¼ mile)

Climb uphill towards the Tor until you reach a ditch. Follow the ditch left. When you come to a wall, follow it up the slope. The Pixies' House can be seen off to your right among tumbled boulders.

THE LEGEND

Crossing described the Pixies' Cave or House as 'a dark-looking cleft close to the ground', and goes on: 'A few years ago this little chamber was capable of holding several persons, but latterly the rocks have gradually moved forward and it is now much smaller than it was. It is not advisable to endeavour to enter it'. The cave appears now as a low, broad opening under a massive slab of rock. Some attempt has been made to fence off the interior by embedding a row of stones in the turf beneath the entrance, but it is certainly pretty uninviting inside, the space cramped, the floor muddy and the walls extremely low. However, at the rear there are signs of a tunnel leading further underground, though it is now too narrow to be negotiated.

Stories of underground tunnels with concealed entrances leading to secret chambers in the heart of the mountains are widespread in British folklore - a faint memory, perhaps, of prehistoric barrows in which, at the far end of narrow stone-slabbed passages, Bronze Age chieftains lay interred, surrounded by their worldly wealth - gold torques and bracelets, amulets of jet or amber, swords, axes and spearheads. Such sites were haunted by the pixies - not the mischievous 'little people' of latter-day fairy tales, but the aboriginal inhabitants of the island - called in Irish mythology the Tuatha de Danaan, the Firbolgs and the Fomorians - driven from their territory by the invading Celts. Such peoples, credited with sinister magical powers, must have lingered on in remote fastnesses like Dartmoor long after the invaders had established themselves in more hospitable areas. According to legend the Pixies' House on the slope of Sheeps Tor - the cave itself - marks the entrance, or antechamber, to such an underground refuge. One story suggests that the midnight watcher will witness the appearance of its spectral inhabitants as they emerge to roam the moor, and that if he or she enters the cave he or she will be seized by invisible hands and carried down into the darkness; another that anyone who succeeds in penetrating to the inner chamber will find a band of prehistoric warriors lying spell-bound upon the stone floor, bronze swords in hand, awaiting the magic command which will release them from their age-long slumber.

Note: A more recent legend also pertains to the spot. Crossing relates that 'one of the Elfords' (a Cavalier family) 'found refuge here during the Civil War, but there is nothing to support the story further than that, about a century ago, some paintings were to be seen on the rocky walls of the cave which were said to be the work of the fugitive'.

HUNTER'S TOR
LUSTLEIGH CLEAVE

THE PHANTOM LEGION

LOCATION

OS 1:25000 Outdoor Leisure Map, North Sheet 28b: Grid Ref. 762824
2.5 km./ 1½ miles NW of LUSTLEIGH; 4 km./2 miles SSW of MORETONHAMPSTEAD

APPROACH BY ROAD

From BOVEY TRACEY (8 km./5 miles): take the A382 Moretonhampstead road then turn left for Lustleigh. Go through the village to the T-junction. Turn right (for N. Bovey), drive past Waye Farm and park by the iron fence.

ACCESS (1.5 km./1 mile)

The path to Hunter's Tor is on your left, along a gulley and up a wooded slope. Bear right near the top and continue along the path with Lustleigh Cleave down to your left until you reach the tor.

THE LEGEND

Hunter's Tor Fort, according to Pevsner (see page 17), was constructed by Iron Age invaders to mark the frontier between them and the native moor-folk' and is one of a chain (see DEWERSTONE ROCK) of such defensive works crowning hill-tops and cliffs along the south and east borders of Dartmoor. Local tradition, however, states that the spot is haunted not by Gauls or 'native moor-folk', but by a troop of Roman legionaries. The phantom soldiers, in full military dress and with standards borne aloft, are seen advancing up the hillside in close formation towards the segment of the rampart which overlooks Lustleigh Cleave. The manifestations only appear on bright moonlit nights: the figures are translucent, and glimmer palely among the scrub and boulders of the slope. It is also said that the cries of battle can be faintly discerned from above but that the defending forces are never seen, the enclosure within the ramparts remaining silent and deserted throughout the occurrence.

One can only assume that Hunter's Tor Fort was reoccupied by Gaulish troops in an attempt to stem the advancing Romans as the latter drove westwards, and that a battle took place at the site between these two peoples. Certainly there is evidence that the Romans passed nearby, for a Roman road led NW from Exeter via the NE borders of Dartmoor to North Tawton and possibly beyond. It may be of relevance that a curious relic of late Roman date, a stone inscribed DATUIDOCI CONHINOCI FILIUS ('the stone of Datuidoc, the son of Conhinoc') can be seen in Lustleigh Church, where it is used as a door-sill in the south porch. Also, Lustleigh churchyard has, according to Woods (*Dartmoor Stone,* 1988), 'all the features of an early Christian burial ground': so we can say with certainty that the area to the east of the fort was eventually settled by Roman or Romano-British communities.

Note: A second legend also pertains to the spot, for it is said that a party of huntsmen wearing Tudor costume and accompanied by a pack of hounds has been seen riding up Lustleigh Cleave or suddenly appearing at the summit as the group breasts the slope of the tor. The phantoms always appear in broad daylight and at the height of summer, and are glimpsed only for an instant before they vanish. It would be convenient to be able to dismiss such sightings as hallucinations brought about by the heat-haze (particularly intense here during hot summer days) and by vague memories of the 'rival' Roman story: but place-names often point to very ancient local traditions, and one wanders how 'Hunter's Tor' originally came by its odd appellation.

CHAW GULLY MINE, CHALLACOMBE DOWN

SUBTERRANEAN DEMONS

LOCATION

OS 1:25000 Outdoor Leisure Map, North Sheet 28b: Grid Ref. 688808
9 km./5 miles SW of MORETONHAMPSTEAD; 4 km./2 miles NE of POSTBRIDGE

APPROACH BY ROAD

From MORETONHAMPSTEAD (9 km./5 miles): take the B3212 (signposted Postbridge and Princetown) onto the open moor. Continue until you reach, on the left, the car park at King's Oven. Park here.

ACCESS (1.5 km./1 mile)

Take the track by the line of telegraph poles down into the valley. Cross the stream at the bottom and follow the path straight ahead of you uphill until you come to the corner of a wall. Here, fork right and follow the lower wall; at the far corner, bear left between spoil heaps and continue until you come to the tree-filled cleft of an old adit.

THE LEGEND

This whole area is scarred by blocked shafts and levels, gullies and spoil-heaps - all evidence of the tin-mining industry which flourished here from ancient times till within living memory. Behind you in the valley lie the remains of Vitiver Mine; to the north, Birch Tor; to the south, among the trees of the pine plantation, Golden Dagger; and above you, beneath the north-west facing slope of Challacombe Down, the deep ravine of Chaw (i.e. 'Chough' or 'Crow') Gully, also termed locally the 'Roman' mine on account of its antiquity. The 'curious circular shaft, cased with stone in the manner of a well ... to be seen in Chaw Gully' (Crossing) no longer exists: according to Woods (*Dartmoor Stone*) it was 'highly dangerous. Only a few broken wires protected the unwary from falling in and it came as a relief to see it filled in'. The adit at whose entrance you have arrived was dug to act as a drainage tunnel, and at its mouth you can still hear after heavy rain the hollow roar of water far underground.

Most Dartmoor tin-bearing lodes also contain small amounts of gold, and Chaw Gully Mine was apparently particularly rich in this precious metal. In its hidden depths lie mounds of gold nuggets which can never be won, as evil creatures haunt the labyrinth of subterranean galleries beneath, standing guard over their secret treasure. In the old days, it is said, foolhardy adventurers seeking to retrieve these hoards occasionally attempted to descend its shafts on the end of a rope; but as they swung down into the darkness a hand would emerge from some concealed side passage, severing their lifeline and plunging the climbers to their death. Next morning, as a grim warning to others, their corpses would be found stretched on the heather by the mouth of the shaft. Belief in the existence of misshapen malevolent beings haunting mine-workings is widespread and of immense antiquity: ancient Chaldean mythology refers to them and they abound in Teutonic folklore. The Kobbolds of Grimm's folktales, Milton's 'Goblins or swart fairies of the Mine', Wagner's Nibelungen and Tolkien's Orcs all derive from a common source. On Dartmoor these goblins are termed 'Knockers': it is said that, on windless nights, the tapping of their hammers can be heard echoing from the mouths of long-abandoned shafts, levels and adits - and that occasionally mortal people encounter them as they emerge from these gloomy openings in the rock to roam the moor during the hours of darkness.

KING WAY, SOURTON TORS

THE GHOST OF LADY HOWARD

LOCATION

OS 1:25000 Outdoor Leisure Map, North Sheet 28b: Grid Ref. 547896
7 km./4 miles SW of OKEHAMPTON; 1.5 km./1 mile SE of SOURTON

APPROACH BY ROAD

From OKEHAMPTON (7 km./4 miles): follow the A386 for Tavistock, turning right onto the dual carriage-way. At the first roundabout, turn left along the A386. When you reach Sourton, turn left by the green and park.

ACCESS (1.5 km./1 mile)

Walk past the church and across the bridge. Climb the track beyond, skirting the north end of Sourton Tors, then turning south to follow the ruts of the old King Way over the shoulder of the hill. As it descends, the track is intersected by a 'reave', before continuing uphill along a narrow gulley between scattered boulders.

THE LEGEND

Over these bleak, desolate moorland uplands ran, in the old days, the main highway from Tavistock to Okehampton. Even in Crossing's day the King Way had long been abandoned, its route in places doubtful and its surface buried beneath encroaching turf and heather (see GIBBET HILL). However, part of its course can still be traced by following a faint track from Nodden Gate (NE of Lydford), past Sourton Tors and down to the village of Meldon. The stretch by Sourton Tors, remote yet accessible, is particularly well-defined.

Lady Howard, of Fitzford House near Tavistock, a famous Jacobean beauty, is alleged to have caused the death of two of her four husbands by poisoning, and to have treated her daughter with extreme cruelty. As a punishment for these crimes, each night her ghost is doomed to travel the old road from Tavistock to Okehampton Castle (where a path winding through the wood at the base of the keep is still named Lady Howard's Walk). Plucking a single blade of grass from the castle lawns she returns home with her trophy, but until the grounds are plucked bare her restless spirit can never find peace. According to some versions of the story she assumes the appearance of a huge black hound, which is seen running beside a skeleton coach. This coach of bones (the bones of her murdered husbands), its ribs gleaming white in the moonlight, is driven by a headless coachman and drawn by four black horses. According to others, including that related by Baring-Gould (*Songs of the West*), the phantom - a corpse-like figure swathed in funereal black - sits huddled inside the coach:

My Ladye hath a sable coach
With horses two and four;
My Ladye hath a gaunt blood-hound
That goeth on before.
My Ladye's coach hath nodding plumes;
The driver hath no head.
My Ladye is an ashen white
As one that long is dead.

In either case, in spite of its headlong speed the coach rushes past in utter silence. No clattering hoofs, no jingling brass or creaking leather, no grind and rattle of iron-shod wheels over stone, are ever heard; and no marks of its passage are cut in the turf.

COFFIN WOOD, CATALOO STEPS

THE PATH OF THE DEAD

LOCATION

OS 1:25000 Outdoor Leisure Map, North Sheet 28b: Grid Ref. 541811
4 km./2 miles ENE of MARY TAVY; 5 km./3 miles SE of LYDFORD

APPROACH BY ROAD

From TAVISTOCK (10 km./6 miles): take the A386 Okehampton road, then turn right for Peter Tavy. Drive through the village and up the narrow road past the 'no through road' sign. Park at the end beyond the gate.

ACCESS (1 km./½ mile)

Follow the Lichway/Willsworthy path down, over the stile, between stone walls and past Brousentor Farm. Continue down a metalled track, then bear left through a gate. Follow the stream down until you come to the River Tavy. Walk along its left bank until you reach the trees of Coffin Wood, which rise steeply to your left as you approach Cataloo Steps.

THE LEGEND

At one time it was compulsory for all the inhabitants of Lydford Parish to be interred in Lydford churchyard and nowhere else. Lydford Parish - the largest in England - covers much of the Forest of Dartmoor and includes a number of isolated farms (known as the Ancient Tenements) scattered far to the east. The deceased of these settlements thus had to be transported across the moor for burial and the route they took is known as the Lych Path (or Lichway). Much of its course has now been obliterated, but its line can still be followed west from Bellever Bridge, then south of Lakehead Hill and across Higher Cherrybrook Bridge to the ridge above Wistman's Wood (see CROCKERN TOR). Between Wistman's Wood and the ford over the Cowsic its course is doubtful, but west of the ford there still exists a grassy track leading past Wittabarrow, then striking NW to Baggator Gate - where you have parked your car - and so to the river crossing by Coffin Wood at Cataloo Steps. From Willsworthy Farm on the west bank of the Tavy 'the path cannot be traced, but it is met with again at Forstall Cross' (Crossing). The eastern section of the Lych Path, however, has not been used for its original purpose since 1260, when Bishop Bronescombe of Exeter, realising the problem ('Et quod loca predicta a matrice ecclesia de Lideford sereno tempore per octo, et tempestatibus exortis in circuitu per quindecim, distant miliaria'), decreed that Widecombe Church might be used instead of Lydford: and so the inhabitants of the Ancient Tenements were permitted 'omnia in vita et morte ecclesiastica percipiant sacramenta in ecclesia de Wydecombe'.

How did Coffin Wood acquire its sinister name? Until the coming of the turnpikes, tracks and paths were the only means of crossing the high moor. The deceased had therefore to be transported to their burial-place in Lydford churchyard slung over the saddle of a packhorse or borne on a litter from the remote farmsteads where they had died. It seems that the body would be carried in this manner as far as Coffin Wood, where a party of pall-bearers (forewarned of its approach by a horseman) would await its arrival with an empty coffin. Below Coffin Wood the transaction would take place: the corpse would be placed in the coffin, then borne across the river and so on to Lydford - hence the name given to this clump of trees. It is said that on certain stormy nights flames - as if from torches - flicker in the gloomy recesses of the wood; the sound of whispering is heard and shadowy figures, bearing a macabre burden, emerge from the trees to keep their ghostly tryst with the dead.

CRAZYWELL POOL, RADDICK HILL

THE DEATH-CALL

LOCATION

OS 1:25000 Outdoor Leisure Map, South Sheet 28a: Grid Ref. 583705
7 km./4 miles NE of YELVERTON; 3 km./1½ miles SSW of PRINCETOWN

APPROACH BY ROAD

From YELVERTON (5 km./3 miles): take the B3212 for Princetown. Turn right in Dousland (for Sheepstor and Burrator) and continue until you come to the reservoir. Carry straight on by the reservoir, following the signs for Car Park and Norsworthy Bridge. Park beyond the bridge.

ACCESS (2 km./1 mile)

Take the track between stone walls which leads off to the right, keeping the fields to your right and the trees to your left, then go through a gate onto the open moor. A little beyond the gate you will come to a deep gulley leading down from the left. Climb this until you reach the Pool.

THE LEGEND

While there is some evidence that Crazywell (or Classenwell) Pool was originally a natural formation, there is no doubt that its present appearance is the result of human activity. It was certainly at least enlarged at some time for use as an industrial reservoir to supply nearby tin mines with water for 'panning' the ore. Once popularly believed to be bottomless - it was said that 'the bellropes belonging to Walkhampton Church were once tied together and let down into it, and yet no bottom was found' (Crossing) - its depth is in fact no more than about fifteen feet. It was also said to rise and fall with the Plymouth tides: this is nonsense, but the water level in the pool does change with surprising speed in times of heavy rain or drought.

A somewhat muddled (and probably fanciful) tradition associates Crazywell Pool with Piers Gaveston, the fourteenth century favourite of Edward II. The story goes that the King's minion, who had retired to the Moor in disgrace, was summoned in a dream to appear one summer dawn by the waters of the pool. Obeying the command he journeyed to the spot and at the appointed hour encountered the Witch of Sheeps Tor. She prophesied that 'his humbled head would soon he high', an ambiguous prediction which Gaveston took to mean he would soon be back in favour, but which in fact foretold his own execution. He was subsequently beheaded and his severed head exhibited on the walls of Warwick Castle. The only 'hard' piece of evidence to support this legend is the historical fact that Gaveston was granted the Wardenship of Dartmoor by his lover-king as a gift. However, Sheeps Tor is supposedly haunted by supernatural forces (see PIXIES' HOUSE) and lies not far to the SW. Also, from the name 'Crazy Well' we can infer that a sacred well or spring perhaps existed there from prehistoric times until it was destroyed by the miners' excavations. In any case the local population regarded the gloomy waters and high encircling banks of Crazywell Pool with superstitious dread. Moorland workers would make a long and exhausting detour to avoid passing close to the spot especially during the hours of dusk or dawn, for it was at these times that, borne upon the wind as it moaned in the hollow and rippled the dark surface of the water, a ghostly voice might be heard calling out the name of the next person in the neighbourhood to die. It is also said that at midnight on Midsummer Eve the face of the next person in Walkhampton Parish to die can be seen in its still waters - so if you happen to be there on that particular date, avoid seeing your own reflection in the pool.

CHILDE'S TOMB, FOXTOR MIRE

SPECTRAL CORTEGE

LOCATION

OS 1:25000 Outdoor Leisure Map, South Sheet 28a: Grid Ref. 624703
5 km./3 miles SE of PRINCETOWN; 4 km./2 miles SW of HEXWORTHY

APPROACH BY ROAD

From PRINCETOWN (3.5 km./2 miles): take the turning by the Methodist chapel along the by-road, following the road round to the right past the 'no through road' sign. Park by the bridge over the Devonport leat.

ACCESS (1.5 km./1 mile)

In order to avoid the marshy expanse of Foxtor Mire it is necessary to make a wide detour round the head of the valley. Follow the Devonport leat downstream along its left bank until you come to the second intake wall running down to your left. Follow this wall, keeping below it, until you see the site, a granite cross surmounting a rough stone plinth, ahead of and below you to your left.

THE LEGEND

Childe's Tomb was considered by Risdon (*A Survey of the County of Devon,* 1630) to be 'one of the three remarkable things to be seen on Dartmoor'. Beneath the cross lie the remains of a Bronze Age kistvaen, or burial chamber; the plinth and cross are said by tradition to mark the spot where 'Childe the Hunter' met his tragic end. The monument - originally standing on three octagonal steps - was dismantled early in the nineteenth century to provide building stone but has since been restored to its present appearance.

Were it not for one curious circumstance, Childe's Tomb would hardly merit a mention in these pages. The legend of the mediaeval 'Childe' (from the Saxon 'cild', or 'lord') out hunting with a party of companions, separated from them during a blizzard and dying of exposure on this desolate spot is familiar to the point of tedium. It is said that before succumbing to the cold he was able to write a will in his own blood, leaving his estates at Plymstock to whichever church gave him burial. The monks of Tavistock found the frozen corpse and (successfully evading a rival group from Plymstock) carried it back to their abbey, thus gaining possession of the dead nobleman's rich legacy. The story, based on historical fact (the original 'Childe' seems to have been a Saxon lord called Ordulf), apparently contains no supernatural element. However, solitary walkers, pony-trekkers, and in one recent instance a car full of tourists driving along the lane to Whiteworks, have witnessed in the area, usually at dusk and in conditions of poor visibility, the following strange supernatural manifestation: a procession of monks carrying a bier emerges briefly from the mist or drizzle; the sound of plainsong chant is borne upon the wind; then gradually the grey-clad figures seem to dissolve and fade away into vacancy, leaving the landscape deserted once more.

Note (1): It is generally accepted that Foxtor Mire was Conan Doyle's model for the Great Grimpen Mire in *The Hound of the Baskervilles,* where the evil Stapleton met his death as he attempted to escape from Holmes and Watson by following his secret path between the pools and swamps which still render the area dangerous after periods of heavy rain.

Note (2): A stone cross standing about one kilometre west of the site marks the line of an ancient monks' path leading from Buckland to the eastern side of the Moor. Perhaps this has some bearing on the story.

GIBBET HILL, BLACK DOWN

THE IRON CAGE

LOCATION

OS 1:25000 Outdoor Leisure Map, North Sheet 28b: Grid Ref. 502811
8 km./5 miles N of TAVISTOCK; 3.5 km./2 miles S of LYDFORD

APPROACH BY ROAD

From TAVISTOCK (8 km./5 miles): take the A386 Okehampton road through Mary Tavy and past the bulk of Gibbet Hill which stands above you to the left. Continue past the Wheal Betsy engine house down to your right and park on the left 100m. or so beyond.

ACCESS (1 km./½ mile)

From the car park you can climb (up a long but fairly easy slope over short turf) direct to the summit, which is marked by a stone pillar.

THE LEGEND

The ancient King Way linking Tavistock and Okehampton (see KING WAY), followed the route of the present road pretty closely over the eastern slope of Gibbet Hill between Mary Tavy and Watervale. According to Crossing 'on the down it has often been come upon by those engaged in repairing the road when they have had occasion to remove surface turf nearby. It ran parallel to it, and not many yards from its western side ... The hill obtains its name from the hideous object said once to have been erected here. The road over the down, which was the direct route from New Bridge on the Tamar to Exeter, had the evil reputation of being infested with highwaymen, and this hill being in view from it, and indeed from the surrounding country, was deemed a fitting place on which to expose the bodies of malefactors who had suffered at the hands of the law ... There are those now living in the parish whose fathers remembered when a tall post was fixed on the summit of the hill'.

Of the 'many traditions and stories concerning the spot' that Crossing mentions, there is one which makes Gibbet Hill worthy of inclusion in these pages. The gruesome practice of hanging the corpse of an executed felon from a gallows as a warning to others continued until well into the nineteenth century. Gibbet Hill was particularly appropriate for this purpose: in a commanding position; close to a busy highway yet on a lonely stretch of its route; and in an area where highway robbery was rife. Inevitably, it drew to itself a number of chilling legends and acquired an extremely sinister reputation - for instance it is probable that witches gathered at the spot in order to steal the corpses, which were employed for potions and other black magic rituals. One source suggests that Gibbet Hill was the site of a form of punishment so barbaric as almost to beggar belief, were the story not supported by local tradition. Apparently from the arm of this particular gibbet dangled an iron cage, into which the condemned malefactor was placed while still alive. Here he hung until exposure, hunger and thirst brought a welcome end to his suffering, his cries ringing out over the surrounding countryside until he became too weak to make himself heard. It is said that, on stormy nights when the wind howls round Gibbet Hill and booms in the valley beneath, a listener on the summit may hear above the soft creaking of chains and a hoarse whispering voice calling over and over again for water or the merciful quietus of a dagger-blow.

WATCHING PLACE, BEETOR CROSS

THE MUFFLED SHAPE

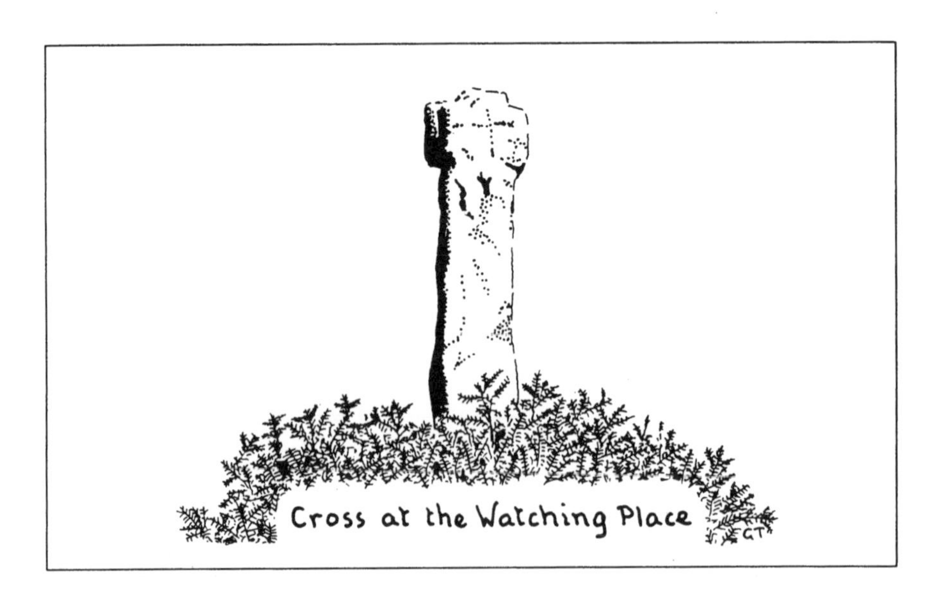

LOCATION

OS 1:25000 Outdoor Leisure Map, North Sheet 28b: Grid Ref 713841
4.5 km./2 1/2 miles SW of MORETONHAMPSTEAD; 8 km./5 miles NE of POSTBRIDGE

APPROACH BY ROAD

From MORETONHAMPSTEAD (4.5 km./2 1/2 miles): take the B3212 Postbridge and Princetown road until you reach the point where the B3344 (signposted Manaton) turns off to the left. This is Beetor Cross, also known locally as Watching Place: the latter name is written on the vertical shaft of the sign-post. To park, drive back along the road for a few metres, where there is a lay-by on the left.

ACCESS

You're there!

THE LEGEND

What is the origin of the strange name given to this apparently innocuous spot? Crossing mentions that 'this part' (of the B3212) 'was once the haunt of a mysterious individual named John Fall, who seems to have been a highwayman with a penchant for frightening his victims by a kind of Spring-heel Jack performance'. Secondly, an ancient cross, 'erected ... to mark the track across the moor on the line of which the present road runs, will be seen in the hedge' (Crossing) by the turning. And thirdly, he goes on to say that 'this spot was also known as Watching Place, and it is said that a gibbet was once erected here, the criminal whose corpse was hanged upon it being the last to be made such an example of in the neighbourhood'.

If one discounts as irrelevant the presence of the nearby cross, there are three possible explanations for the strange name given to this locality. Perhaps 'Watching Place' was so called because it was here that highwaymen lay in wait for their victims; or maybe the relatives and friends of the hanged man watched over the corpse to protect it from theft by witches. The corpses of condemned malefactors were considered to be very efficacious in certain black magic rituals: the witches in Shakespeare's *Macbeth*, for instance, throw 'grease that's sweaten/From the murderer's gibbet' into the fire beneath their cauldron; and the 'Hand of Glory', that used to bring about the death of an enemy, consisted of the severed hand of such a corpse clutching a candle made from its hair and fat. However, another tradition suggests that when an outbreak of plague struck a nearby house in mediaeval times, food for the inhabitants was left on a granite slab at the spot, the charitable donors 'watching' from a safe distance to ascertain that the afflicted were still alive. When the gifts remained uncollected and it was evident that the victims were dead or dying, the house, with the plague-ridden corpses within, was burnt to the ground as a disinfectant measure. Watching Place is said to be haunted by a cloaked and hooded figure which stands in an attitude of mourning beside the shaft of the signpost. One recent encounter with this spectre was experienced by the driver of a car who passed the spot late one night during a violent rainstorm. Seeing the figure - a vague, muffled shape in the gloom - he assumed it was waiting for the Moretonhampstead bus and stopped to offer a lift. He wound his window down and called across, whereupon the phantom raised its head and fixed the terrified driver with glaring-red, empty sockets where the eyes should have been.

HANGMAN'S PIT, COMBESTONE TOR

SAMUEL HUNNAFORD'S GHOST

LOCATION

OS 1:25000 Outdoor Leisure Map, South Sheet 28a: Grid Ref. 672715
8.5 km./5 miles SE of PRINCETOWN; 8.5 km./5 miles NW of ASHBURTON

APPROACH BY ROAD

From ASHBURTON (9 km./5 miles): follow the signs for Holne but by-pass the village by taking the Hexworthy road across Venford dam. Hangman's Pit is situated about a kilometre beyond the dam, to the right of the road and below some iron railings. Park on the grass verge to the left of the road and a few metres beyond the site.

ACCESS

You're there!

THE LEGEND

Crossing describes Hangman's Pit as 'a deep hollow running down to the Dart.... The work of the tin-seeker is abundantly evident, but grass and heather now cover the heaps he cast up, and the mountain ash grows in the sheltered nooks that these form'. A stream runs down through the cleft and the bottom is weed-grown and marshy, but the rowans are still there, clinging to its steep sides.

Why is Hangman's Pit so called? Crossing again: 'A moorman who lived at Round Hill, near Two Bridges, was returning from Brent Fair, where he had changed his horse for another, and finding, it was supposed, that he had the worst of the bargain, was so troubled at what he had done that on arriving at the hollow he determined to take his life. He was found hanging from one of the trees amid the stone heaps, and on being cut down the body was taken to a barn at Hexworthy ... About the time when it was thought he must have committed the rash act his wife imagined she saw him approaching the door of their house'. Later research has established that the incident occurred in 1826, that the man's name was Samuel Hunnaford, and that he used his horse's halter to hang himself from one of the rowans growing from the sides of the pit. It also seems that he was cheated by a gypsy, exchanging his own horse for another (which proved to be lame) and a small sum of money. Too ashamed of his gullibility to face his wife and family, the wretched man choked his life out in this remote, desolate gulley. The strange hallucination his wife experienced when she imagined she saw (or in some versions of the story, heard) him arriving home at the very moment of his death is particularly interesting in view of the nature of this haunting, for it seems that sometimes extremely violent destructive emotions - despair or rage - have the power to 'imprint' themselves on the surrounding landscape, and that these 'vibrations' can still be picked up by the psychically sensitive long after the original incident occurred. Such may well be the case with regard to the ghost of Samuel Hunnaford, for it is said that this phantom horseman rides down into Hangman's Pit at midnight, pauses as if deep in thought, then emerges from the hollow and continues on his way along the road in the direction of Round Hill. This haunting, then, appears to be the psychic projection of a terrible mental struggle: the ghost enacts what the man had originally intended to do - should indeed have done had he not succumbed to his mood of suicidal despair.

STEPHENS' GRAVE, WHITE TOR

THE GREY GHOST

Stephen's Grave

LOCATION

OS 1:25000 Outdoor Leisure Map, North Sheet 28b: Grid Ref. 536781
3.5 km./2 miles SE of MARY TAVY; 2 km./1 mile E of PETER TAVY

APPROACH BY ROAD

From TAVISTOCK (6 km./3 miles): take the B3357 Princetown road, turning left for Peter Tavy. Drive through the village and past the church, then take the first right turn (signposted No Through Road). Park in the quarry.

ACCESS (1.5 km./1 mile)

Take the left fork along the bridle-path to Stephens' Grave/White Tor. The pillar marking the site of the grave stands out in the open moor to the right of the track and at the point where the moor is crossed by a faint path running north-south.

THE LEGEND

Described by Crossing merely as a 'mound', Stephens' Grave is now marked by a rough pillar of black basalt surmounting a triangular plinth inscribed with the letter S. He goes on: 'Stephens' Grave ... marks the site where a suicide was buried with the barbarous rites once customary. George Stephens was a youth of Peter Tavy, and was driven to take his life by the unfaithfulness of the girl to whom he was betrothed. It is said that at the moment he was laid here some linen that was hanging out to bleach at Higher Godsworthy' (a farm to the SW across the valley) 'was caught up in the air and never more seen'. To this bare account can be added the following: George (or John, according to some sources) Stephens committed suicide by taking poison in October 1762, perhaps (as Crossing suggests) because his fiancée betrayed him with another; other versions maintain that he did so because she spurned his advances, or because her parents rejected him as an appropriate suitor for their daughter's hand. According to yet another tradition he murdered the unfortunate girl by presenting her with a poisoned apple, afterwards partaking of it himself.

Suicides were not only refused full Christian burial rites: the sites chosen for such interments always lay at the farthest extremity of the parish in which the victim lived and usually at a cross-roads. In some instances the corpse was also tranfixed with a wooden stake through the heart. Some at least of these precautions (designed to deter the spirit of the dead person from returning to haunt those whom it held responsible for its tragic fate) were evidently taken in the case of the site under investigation: for Stephens' Grave lies out on the open moor, far from human habitation and at a point where two paths cross. Local tradition asserts that the ghost - a pale skeletal form swathed in the tattered remains of a grey shroud - patrols the cross-paths on misty nights, making little darting runs to and fro as if blindly seeking the way home and uttering shrill cries of anguish. Those who have encountered it at close quarters report that the face is skull-like, the skin stretched dry and withered over protruding cheek-bones and each sunken eye-socket concealed beneath a dusty net or pad of cobwebs.

Note: The reputedly Neolithic fort on the summit of nearby White Tor is also worth a visit. Stories concerning the site are vague and it has not been possible to obtain any direct evidence of supernatural occurrences, but it seems that the camp may be haunted by its aboriginal inhabitants.

THE BROAD STONES, ROWBROOK

THE CRY OF THE DART

LOCATION

OS 1:25000 Outdoor Leisure Map, South Sheet 28a: Grid Ref. 689723
7 km./4 miles NW of ASHBURTON; 2 km./1 mile SE of DARTMEET

APPROACH BY ROAD

From ASHBURTON (8 km./5 miles): follow the signs for Dartmeet over Holne and New Bridges, through Poundsgate and past a right turn to Corndon. A few metres beyond you come to Bel Tor car park on your left. Park here.

ACCESS (1.5 km./1 mile)

At the far left corner of the car park take the track between stone walls. Follow this, then bear right by the Nature Reserve sign and continue downhill until you arrive at a brook (Simon's Lake) running down from your right. Follow this down till you reach the Dart. The Broad Stones - a jumble of boulders jutting into the river - lie just downstream.

THE LEGEND

One peculiar feature of the Dart is the almost uncanny speed with which its water level rises and falls during spells of wet or dry weather: the thin top-soil of the moor, the absence of tree cover and underlying impervious granite - combined with the sudden downpours for which the area is notorious - mean that rain-water, instead of soaking into the ground, is released almost immediately into the river system. Formations such as the Broad Stones - dry under normal conditions - can therefore become totally inundated in a matter of minutes. Also, the sinister roar of the torrent in spate as it rushes over and round the boulders in its bed after heavy rain can be heard at some considerable distance. It may well be that this latter phenomenon is - at least partly - responsible for the legend of Jan Coo. I suspect that the origins of this legend are extremely ancient, and possibly derive from a time when natural features such as lakes or rivers were believed each to be inhabited by its own presiding deity. It is easy to see how primitive man, at the mercy of flood or drought, came to regard these mysterious forces as capricious supernatural beings to be feared and therefore worshipped. In prehistoric times such 'gods' were propitiated by human sacrifice; later, suicides and even accidental drownings were accepted with a certain fatalistic satisfaction, for when the river had taken its victim others might feel safer for a while. And the old rhyme,

Dart, Dart, cruel Dart
Every year thou claim'st a heart

- still current in the neighbourhood - is further evidence of the superstition that the Dart continues to demand its annual human sacrifice; a more modern variation of the legend maintains that 'the cry o' the Brad Stones' - the voice of the river itself, the roar of flood water as it cascades over the boulders - is a sure sign of imminent foul weather. All these elements come together in the story of Jan Coo, a young farm labourer from nearby Rowbrook who, night after night over a period of weeks, heard the cry of the Dart summoning him to his death. After a while he could withstand the call no longer. Convinced he was destined to become the river's next victim he ran from the house shouting 'Dart's calling me!' and disappeared into the darkness. He was never seen again; nor - strangely - was his body ever found. The Broad Stones, then, are haunted by a crying voice, either the voice of the Dart summoning another victim, or the spectral voice of Jan Coo himself.

GREEN COMBE, CHALLACOMBE CROSS

HAUNTED BRIDGE

LOCATION

OS 1:25000 Outdoor Leisure Map, North Sheet 28b: Grid Ref. 694829
6 km./3 miles NE of POSTBRIDGE; 6.5 km./4 miles SW of MORETONHAMPSTEAD

APPROACH BY ROAD

From MORETONHAMPSTEAD (6.5 km./4 miles): take the B3212 towards Postbridge and Princetown) past the turnings at Beetor Cross (signposted Manaton - see WATCHING PLACE) and Challacombe Cross (signposted Widecombe). Just beyond Challacombe the road descends steeply to cross a stream. There is a level area by the stream to the left where you may park.

ACCESS

You're there already!

THE LEGEND

The ghost of Green Combe, where the headwaters of the East Bovey River pass under the road, seems to be associated with the series of hauntings which bedevil the B3212 from Moretonhampstead in the east to Rundlestone in the west. Accounts are confused and contradictory, but it seems that from this insignificant spot emanates an atmosphere of horror strong enough to cause passing motorists or cyclists to lose control of their machines. One witness, a woman driving home from Princetown to Moretonhampstead in broad daylight, experienced such a powerful sensation of icy cold as she crossed the bridge that, thinking she must have caught a touch of flu, she parked her car by the roadside in order to put on her coat, which lay on the rear seat. Her dog, which was also on the rear seat, was lying in an extremity of terror - shivering, whining, its hackles up and teeth bared. In this instance nothing untoward was actually seen, but other motorists (and cyclists) have reported that, as they descend the slope in either direction, some creature appears beside the vehicle and runs beside it, waving its arms in a frantic manner as if to warn of some danger ahead. The figure is glimpsed only out of the corner of the eye, and so descriptions of it are vague in the extreme: it is said to be of human shape, though no larger than a child, and its outlines are shadowy and ill-defined. Some witnesses say that it seems to be clad in a pale tattered shroud or cloak that flutters in the wind as it runs, and that the general effect is of a hysterical, panic-stricken attempt to overhaul the vehicle it is pursuing. One peculiarity is that the creature always matches its speed with that of the pursued vehicle - bicycle or car - and seems incapable of outrunning it however slowly it is travelling.

I suspect that this legend is an aspect of the extraordinary series of occurrences known collectively as the 'Hairy Hands' - perhaps the oddest, as well as the most notorious, of Dartmoor hauntings. For the past seventy years the B3212 has been the scene of numerous inexplicable accidents: horses bolt, cars skid off the road and overturn; a motor-cycle combination simply disintegrated at speed, killing the driver. Eventually a motor-cyclist who had survived one such incident reported that his machine had been wrenched off the road by a pair of huge, powerful hairy hands closing over his own on the handle-bars. On another occasion a woman sleeping parked in a lay-by on the road near Postbridge was woken one night by a black, ape-like hand clawing at the window; when she made the sign of the cross, it vanished. No explanation for these incidents has ever been found.

JAY'S GRAVE
CRIPDON DOWN

THE KNEELING MOURNER

LOCATION

OS 1:25000 Outdoor Leisure Map, North Sheet 28b: Grid Ref. 733799
6.5 km./4 miles SW of MORETONHAMPSTEAD; 3.5 km./2 miles NE of WIDECOMBE

APPROACH BY ROAD

From MORETONHAMPSTEAD (9.5 km./6 miles): take the B3212 towards Postbridge, then turn left along the B3344 (signposted Manaton). Where the Manaton road turns off left at Heatree cross-roads, continue straight on (signposted Hound Tor, Haytor and Widecombe) over the cattle grid and past the telephone kiosk. A little further on, opposite a public bridleway sign and on the edge of a wood, you will come to Jay's Grave by the roadside on your right. Park on the verge beyond the site.

ACCESS

You're there!

THE LEGEND

This 'pathetic little mound' (Crossing) is obviously a grave, a turf-covered rectangular mound ringed with boulders and with a roughly-hewn headstone raised at one end. It is usually adorned with crossed twigs, fresh bouquets of wild flowers and sprays of foliage picked from nearby hedgerows.

Jay's Grave is probably Dartmoor's most famous landmark, and its story is extremely well-known. Some time during the eighteenth century an orphaned child named Kitty Jay was employed on a farm at Manaton, where she was seduced, became pregnant and - abandoned by her lover and persecuted by local opinion - committed suicide by hanging herself in one of the barns at her place of work. Her body was buried, as was customary in such cases (see STEPHENS' GRAVE), not in her local churchyard but at this lonely spot where a footpath crosses the road. Gradually the true facts became obscured until it was generally believed that 'Jay's Grave' contained not human, but animal remains. However, in 1860 one James Bryant of nearby Hedge Barton excavated the site and uncovered the skeleton of a 'young female person'. He placed the bones in a coffin which was re-interred in the same spot, and raised the mound as it appears today. Of the two legends associated with Jay's Grave the more famous (the 'who puts the flowers there?' mystery) is obviously fanciful. Beatrice Chase, the author of *The Heart of the Moor,* seems to have been responsible for the original myth, placing the floral tributes there herself and putting about the story that some supernatural agency had been at work. Since her death others - mostly tourists - have continued the tradition, pausing in their explorations of the moor to adorn the grave with fresh flowers. However another superstition, less widely known and far more credible, also pertains to the spot. It is said that on certain moonlit summer nights a dark figure may be seen kneeling in an attitude of mourning, its head bowed and face buried in its hands, beside the grave. Opinion is divided as to whether the spectre is male or female, for it is heavily muffled in a long black cloak and hood and its outlines are shadowy and ill-defined: but witnesses always stoutly maintain that somehow they 'know' it is not the ghost of Kitty Jay herself. Perhaps the grave is haunted by the unquiet spirit of one of those who drove her to her tragic death; or perhaps the phantom of her faithless lover is doomed to keep eternal vigil over the spot where his victim and their unborn child lie buried.

Note: Heatree House (a little to the north) was most likely Conan Doyle's model for Baskerville Hall. (See also SQUIRE CABELL'S TOMB.) It is now the Heatree House Activity Centre.

BIBLIOGRAPHY

BARBER, Chips: *Dark and Dastardly Dartmoor (Obelisk, Exeter, 1988)*

BARING-GOULD, Rev. Sabine: *A Book of Dartmoor (Methuen, 1900)*
Songs of the West (Methuen, 1895)

BRAY, Mrs A. E.: *Traditions, Legends and Superstitions of Devonshire (John Murray, 1836)*

BRETON, Hugh: *The Forest of Dartmoor (Hoyton & Colt, 1931)*

BUTLER, Jeremy: *Dartmoor Atlas of Antiquities (Devon Books, 1991)*

CHASE, Beatrice: *Dartmoor the Beloved (1951)*
The Heart of the Moor (Herbert Jenkins, 1914)

CROSSING, William T.: *Guide to Dartmoor (1912; repr. Peninsula Press, Newton Abbot, 1990)*
A Hundred Years on Dartmoor (WMN Plymouth 1901, repr. Devon Books 1987)
Tales of the Dartmoor Pixies (W.H.Hood, 1890)

DOONE, Val: *We See Devon*

DOYLE, Sir Arthur Conan: *The Hound of the Baskervilles (1901-2, repr. Octopus 1984)*

FRAZER, Sir James George: *The Golden Bough (Macmillan, 1922)*

GRAVES, Robert: *The White Goddess (Faber & Faber, 1943)*

HEMERY, Eric: *High Dartmoor (Robert Hale, London, 1983)*

HOLE, Christina: *A Mirror of Witchcraft (Pedigree Books, 1957)*
English Folk Heroes

HUGHES, Pennethorne: *Witchcraft (Pelican, 1967)*

LETHBRIDGE, T. C.: *Witches (Routledge & Kegan Paul, 1962)*

LIND, Frank: *My Occult Casebook*

O'DONNELL, G.: *Haunted Waters*

PAGE, J. L.: *Exploration of Dartmoor (Seeley, 1889)*

PEGG, John: *The Magic of the Moor (Dartmoor Magazine 1986)*

PENNICK, Nigel: *Practical Magic in the Northern Tradition (Aquarian Press, 1989)*

PEVSNER, Nikolaus: *The Buildings of England (South Devon) (Penquin, 1952)*

PHILLPOTTS, Eden: *Brunel's Tower*

ST. LEGER-GORDON, D.: *Devonshire (Robert Hale, 1950)*

ST. LEGER-GORDON, Ruth E.: *The Witchcraft and Folklore of Dartmoor (1965; repr. Alan Sutton, Gloucester, 1982)*

SALMON, Arthur: *Dartmoor (Blackie, 1913)*

SUMMERS, Montague: *History of Witchcraft (Univ.Books Inc NY, 1958)*

VARIOUS: *Proceedings of the Society for Psychical Research*
Transactions of the Devonshire Association

WHITLOCK, Ralph: *The Folklore of Devon (Batsford, London, 1977)*

WILSON, Colin: *The Occult (Wayflower, 1975)*

WOODS, Stephen H.: *Dartmoor Stone (Devon Books, 1988)*

WORTH, R. Hansford: *Dartmoor (1953; repr. as Worth's Dartmoor, David & Charles, 1988)*